Wedding Ceremony Planning Book for Couples

A practical step by step guide on how you can plan a successful white wedding

- Plan with any budget

- Suitable for any country

- Suitable for any church

WORLDWIDE WEDDING PLANNING GUIDE

D A Ihenze

Copyright © 2014
D A IHENZE
ISBN-13:978-1533072658
ISBN-10:1533072655
FIRST PUBLISHED IN JUNE 2015

Published in USA by
CREATESPACE PUBLISHERS

Typeset in Nigeria by
TK COMPUTERS
5, Oyenuga Street, Akoka, Yaba, Lagos State, Nigeria

For marketing and distribution enquiry, email
desmondihenze@yahoo.com

Phone number
+234 8038094830

DEDICATION

Wedding comes once in a lifetime.

This book is dedicated to all new couples who are currently planning their weddings all over the world. I wish them happy wedding planning.

ACKNOWLEDGMENTS

I will first of all thank Almighty God who has been my source of inspiration and ideas. I will also thank all those who have provided useful materials that helped to make this manual a successful self guide.

CONTENTS

Wedding Ceremony Functions

Step 1

Before you start planning for wedding

- Make sure that you have studied your partner's character very well and you have become satisfied that he or she would make you happy in your marriage. It will not be proper for you to wed and divorce in future.

- Make sure that your parents/family members and your partner's parents/family members have all agreed that both of you can become husband and wife. There are always problems in any marriage that parents and family members don't consent to.

- Make sure that both of you have undergone blood tests to know your blood groups and genotypes and the results proved that both of you can get married without any problem in your marriage.

Step 2

Do you want to go for traditional or Court wedding also?

- Choose whether you will like to include court wedding or traditional wedding or both depending on the marriage tradition of the bride and your choice.

- If you would like to go for both court and traditional wedding, you can fix the dates on the same day to cut down costs.

- Choose whether you would like to organize a bachelor's eve party for your white wedding. If you wish to organize this, remember that the date should be fixed on the night before your wedding day.

Step 3

Start discussing your white wedding ceremony with people

- Confirm your wedding date with your life partner and fix the date.

- Start discussing your wedding with your partner especially how you want it to be done.

- Discuss it with your own parents and your partner's parents.

- Select the important personalities you want to invite such as your sponsors, chief hosts, father of the day, mother of the day, RSVP etc.

- Discuss your wedding with your priest, pastor or an officiator.

- Discuss it with your close friends and your relations.

- Set a budget for your wedding and decide how expenses will be shared. You can discuss this with your partner and sponsors.

- Pick a special adviser or a wedding specialist if you like and discuss your wedding with him or her.

- Decide and arrange for where you and your partner will live after the wedding.

Step 4

Settlement of conflicts

- Publish your names in the marriage lists in your church.

- Include your names under the bans of marriage.

- If you or your partner offended or disappointed anybody, make sure that you have reconciled with the person before your wedding. Offended or disappointed people can hinder, obstruct or cause confusion on your wedding day.

Step 5

Start getting ready for the wedding day

- Get your blood tests results ready if it is needed.

- Prepare other medical examinations that may be needed ready. Some churches ask for HIV tests results.

- Get your birth certificates ready.

- Get your baptism cards / certificates ready.

- Get other documents or certificates that the priest/pastor/officiator may require ready.

- If you wish to travel out of the country for your honey moon, make plans for it. Prepare your passport, visas and other documents and get them ready.

- Start attending marriage classes and wedding rehearsals or dancing lessons (optional)

Step 6

Choose your wedding guests

- List out the names of the important personalities whose names will be written on invitation card. Also, you can compile and invitation list if you like.

- Make an estimate of the number of people who you want to invite in terms of welfare and seats.

- Choose a reception venue, church, date and time for your wedding

- You can prepare contract forms and important papers for the people you want to give some jobs as contract (optional).

- Make a booking or deposit for the venue or hall where you want the reception to be held.

- Confirm your wedding date with your priest/ pastor / officiator.

- Select an invitation card wording or make your own wording plus card design.

- Prepare directions on the invitation card to guide your guests to the church and reception venue.

- Give your wedding card to a printer to print for you.

- Choose and buy the size and type of envelopes that you will use to distribute the cards. Give the size of the envelopes that you have chosen to your printer to measure the size of the cards.

- Send out invitation cards to your guests at least 4 to 6 weeks in advance.

- You may choose to place wedding announcement in newspaper or other forms of publicity.

Step 7

You may want to print wedding programme booklet

- You and your partner's photo should be printed in front of the programme booklet and also on the other pages of the booklet.

- The Bible readings of the wedding ceremony should be in the programme booklet.

- The hymns to be sung during the church service should be in the booklet.

- The wedding reception programme should be listed in the booklet.

- The order of wedding photography at the church premises can be listed in the booklet.

- The names of your bridal party and workers should be in the booklet. E.g. ring bearer, cake designer, bride's maids, flower girl etc.

Step 8

Select the people who will work with you. Tick the ones you will need.

Officiator /Priest/ Pastor): The person who will join both of you together at the church.

Choir: The people who will sing during the wedding service.

Bride's maids: The single ladies who will go with the bride.

Little Bride/Groom: Children bride & groom.

Chief bride's maid/maid of honor: Special or personal assistant to the bride who will be closer to her.

Flower Girl: A small girl who will carry the flower basket and as well sprinkle the flowers.

Groom's men: The men who will go with the bridegroom.

Best man: Special or personal assistant to the bridegroom.

M.C: The person who will announce the details and items of the wedding ceremony.

Baker: The person who will design the wedding cake.

Caterer: The person who will be in charge of food. A caterer can also design the cake.

Ushers: The people who will welcome and usher people to their seats.

Balloon/Venue decorators: The person who will decorate the car, church and reception venue.

Calligrapher: (Optional) a person who uses special pen to produce beautiful handwriting on invitation cards etc.

Security men: The people who will be in charge of security.

Servers: The people who will serve your guests. Sometimes, the caterer provides the servers.

Arrangers & cleaners: People to be employed to arrange and clean the chairs and tables and keep the Venue neat.

Photographer: The person who will take the wedding photos.

Videographer: The video camera man who will cover the whole occasion.

Make up Artist: The person who will make the bride and others up. (Optional)

Hair Stylist: The person who will design and arrange the bride's hair and others (optional)

Driver: The person who will drive the bride and the bridegroom. Also, drivers who will drive the bridal party.

D.J: The person who will supply music for entertainment.

Live Band Musicians: You can personally employ musicians to play music at the venue for entertainment. (Optional)

Band boys: You can employ band boys to beat bands with flutes. (Optional)

Readers: The people who will read Bible verses during wedding service at the Church. (Optional) Note: The bride and groom are expected to do this.

Ring Bearer: The child who will present the ring.

Florist: A person who will supply flowers that are needed for the occasion. He or she can also design anything or any place that requires flower designs.

Comedians: The people who will entertain the guest and make them laugh. (Optional)

Dancers: The people who will entertain the guests with dances or chorography. (Optional)

Dramatists: The people who can perform short dramas to entertain the guests (optional)

Step 9

Select and tick the items or properties you will need for the wedding

Cars: These will be used to carry the bride / bridegroom and other people to the church, reception and back home. A special car or limousine can be hired for the couple.

Vehicles: Long buses that will be used carry items and some people to the reception venue or church.

Wedding Rings: The rings that will be used to join the bride and bridegroom. Note that some churches use Bible instead of rings. Choose according to your church tradition.

Ring Pillow: A small pillow where the wedding ring will be attached to.

Flower Basket: A small basket that will contain the pieces of flower for the flower girl.

Hand Gloves: To be worn by the bride and bridegroom.

Reception Venue: The place for your reception after church.

Reception Place Cards: (a) small cards that contain the address and details of the reception venue if the venue address is not written on the invitation cards (b) bigger cards used to indicate sitting arrangement.

Bride and Groom's Chairs: Specially designed chairs made for bride and groom to sit at the reception.

Toasting Glasses: To be used at the reception venue.

Cake Knife: For cutting the cake and it is usually produced by the cake baker.

Server Trays/ Sets/ Cake Top: For serving the cake.

Candles/ Candle Holders: (optional).

Bibles: Usually used as special gift for the couple. It can also be used to join the couples.

Guest Book & Pen: The guests who attend your wedding can write down their names and addresses (optional).

Wedding Bells: (Optional)

Bouquet: A bunch of flower made for the bride to carry throughout the wedding ceremony.

Garter: An elastic band that the bride wears round her leg.

Tables/Canopies: (if not available at the venue or hall).

Chairs: For guests (if not available at the hall or venue).

Wedding Favors: Beautiful and specially designed little items that can be given to the guests at the reception.

Linens: For the covering of the tables. You can discuss this with the decorator or caterer.

Drums: For cooling the drinks or you can provide a refrigerator van.

Serving Dishes, Glasses, Utensils: You can discuss this with your caterer or you can personally produce them.

Special Wines, Hots, Gins, Juice: For decorating the table.

Generating Set: This may be needed incase of power failure. You can discuss this with your DJ or you can personally Produce or rent it.

Wishing Bubbles: (optional)

Confetti: Small bits of colored paper thrown by wedding guests at the bride and Groom. (Optional)

Gift for the bride: To be given to the bride by the groom (optional).

Gift for the groom: To be given to the groom by the bride (optional).

Gifts for the bridal party: (optional).

Gifts for the bride's parents: (optional).

Step 10

Select the kind of food that you want your guests to eat

Jollof Rice

Fried or white rice

Melon soup

Vegetable soup

Native soup

MoiMoi

Salad

Pounded yam

Foo foo

Plantain

White rice & stew

Cow meat

Goat meat

Bush meat

Fish

Turkey

Chicken

Note: The foods listed above are just mere suggestions. You can choose foods that you are sure that your guests would like which are not listed above.

Step 11

Welfare Discussion

- Make estimate of the number of people that you are expecting.

- Remember that you must not budget for just the total number of people that you gave invitation cards.

- Many people who you did not invite will come and the people who you invited will also come along with people.

- Choose whether you will hand over the cooking contract to a professional caterer; you can also ask relations, families, villagers, church people, neighbors etc to do the cooking for you.

- If you are using a professional caterer, discuss with her based on the number of people that you are expecting and the kind of food you want.

- Choose whether you would want snacks to be fried and served at the reception venue before the normal food will be served and discuss this with your caterer.

Step 12

Serving your guests

- If you are handing the cooking over to a caterer, she is to produce service boys / girls plus serving dishes.

- If other people are helping you to cook the food, you have to arrange for servers, dishes and spoons.

- You can choose to serve with take away plates and spoons if you want.

- Appoint somebody who is close to you to be in charge of distributing the drinks.

Step 13

Select the kinds of drinks that you want to give to your guests.

Bottled / Sachet water (essential).

Can / Paper Juice

Soft drinks

Beers

Wines

Gins / Hots

Palm wine

Note: The drinks listed above are just mere suggestions. You can choose drinks that you are sure that your guests would like which are not listed above.

Step 14

Purchase or rent your wedding dresses

- Select the kind of tuxedo/ suit and the tie you want to use.

- Tell your best man and groom's men the kind of tuxedo / suit and the tie you want them to use.

- Purchase or rent the wedding gown of the bride with the veil/head piece, shoes and all accessories that accompany the wedding gown. And don't forget the garter.

- Prepare or rent dress for the flower girl, ring bearer, little bride and little groom.

- Prepare or rent dress for the chief bride's maid and her accessories.

- Prepare dresses for bride's maids. They may wish to be responsible for their dresses.

- If necessary or possible, arrange and prepare dresses for the parents of both bride and bridegroom.

- You may wish to select a uniform material, head tie or cap for the invited guests to purchase and use for the wedding.

Step 15

Arrange for wedding favors or take away gifts for your guests

You can choose to give any of these gifts below to your guests. You can also order wedding favors from wedding favor dealers.

1. Umbrellas

2. Buckets

3. Clothing materials.

4. Dishes / cooking utensils.

5. Camera phones

6. Photo cameras

7. Soaps/Detergents

8. Creams

9. Beverages

10. Big Notes/Jotters

11. Calendars

12. Words of wisdom cards

13. Handkerchiefs

14. Can juice

15. Towels

16. Toiletries

17. Bags

18. Special cups

Note: The gifts listed above are just mere suggestions. You can choose the gifts that you are sure that your guests would like which are not listed above.

Step 16

A week to the wedding day assignments

- Arrange for accommodations for out-of town guests.

- Prepare sitting arrangements for your guests. You can indicate each group with card boards which will be pasted or hanged at visible positions.

- Get your wedding programme booklets ready.

- If you are not using programme booklets or you did not print the order of photography on the booklets, prepare it and hand it over to the person who you appointed to read them out.

- Select special songs or music that you want the DJ to play and also tell him when to play them.

- Choose the music that you will want to dance with your wife when you are called out to dance and discuss it with the DJ.

- If you have special music that you want the DJ to play which you believe that he will not have, get the music ready.

- Prepare your **About to Wed** and **Just Wedded** cards to be pasted on car plate numbers on your wedding day.

- If you have special shots or features that you want the videographer to cover, discuss it with him.

- Practice wearing your wedding shoes before the wedding day if they are new shoes. This can be done even before a week to the wedding.

- You can test your wedding dresses before the wedding day and make sure that they fit you.

- Get a small bag and pack some of your emergency dressing items into it. E.g electric iron, needle/ thread, hair spray, a bottle of spirit, aspirin/ panadol, nail polish, safety pins, lip-stick, powder, brush/ comb, cleaning solution etc.

- Arrange for the person who will decorate the cars on wedding day.

Step 17

Do you want Rehearsal Dinner or Bachelor's Eve?

Rehearsal Dinner

This is the rehearsal that takes place the night before the wedding ceremony, with a dinner party to follow. It is your insurance that everything is ready and all your attendants are present and are all informed of their duties.

Bachelor's Eve

This is another event that takes place at the night before the wedding ceremony. It features drinking, dancing, light meal and series of funs. It is the night in which the groom traditionally says good bye to all his girl-friends and dates because he is about to settle down with his life partner.

You can now decide whether you want to organize bachelor's eve, rehearsal dinner, both of them or none of them.

Step 18

A day before the wedding day assignments

- Groom barb your hair neatly.

- Bride dress your hair.

- Contact the wedding party to make sure that they are all well prepared and remind them of anything they forget.

- Wife, send a romantic note to your husband before the ceremony to remind him that you love him.

- If you organized bachelor's night, prepare for it. After it, come home quickly to have a good night's sleep before the wedding and you will be happy.

- Remind the person who you have called to decorate the cars to come very early and do the work.

Step 19

Wedding Day

- Before you get dressed or have make up, take a light break-fast. This is necessary because you may not have the opportunity to eat food until your wedding ceremony is over.

- If your wedding is held during rainy months, go with umbrella incase of emergency.

- Select handkerchief to be kept into your pocket for your own use.

- Remind the wedding party to gather quickly after your vows for group photographs. You will want to greet and acknowledge waiting guests as soon as possible.

- If you're planning on candles, make sure that you have appointed someone to light them.

- If you are using guests register, don't forget to go with the book and place it at the reception.

- Check and make sure that you are going to the church with your wedding rings. Some couples forget their wedding rings at home while going to the church.

- Be sure that **About to Wed** banner has been pasted on the car plate number and arrange for the person who will replace it with **Just Wedded** after the church service.

Step 20

Your wedding ceremony is now going on

Step 21

The next day after the wedding.

- Go to church for thanksgiving for the success of your wedding.

- Getting home from church, you will welcome and entertain visitors and well wishers.

- Some people can still bring wedding gifts to you especially those who could not attend your wedding.

- If you want to go for horny moon, get ready to leave.

Step 22

Three to four days after your wedding

- Send thank you notes/cards to people who honored your invitations and people who gave you wedding gifts.

- You and your wife can also choose to visit them to thank them.

- The wife should publish change of name on newspapers (optional).

- The wife should change her name in bank accounts, loans, credit cards, driver's license, passport, social security and other important documents.

Wedding Ceremony Functions

Function 1
Wedding Vows

Function 2
Wedding Speeches

Function 3
The order of wedding ceremony

Function 4
The order of events at your wedding reception venue

Function 5
Wedding Invitation wording samples

Function 6
Thanking the guests who attended your wedding

Important facts about wedding

How you can remain happy after your wedding

Wedding Vows

Wedding Vow 1

In the name of Jesus, I.....................take you, ..., to be my (husband/wife), to have and to hold, from this day forward, for better, for worse, for richer, for poorer, in sickness and in health, to love and to cherish, for as long as we both shall live. This is my solemn vow.

Wedding Vow 2

I,........................... , take you ...., to be my wedded (husband/wife), to have and to hold from this day forward, for better for worse, for richer for poorer, in sickness and in health, to love and to cherish, 'til death do us part: according to God's holy ordinance, and thereto I pledge you my love and faithfulness.

Wedding Vow 3

I love you................. as I love no other. All that I have I share with you. I take you to be my (husband/wife) through health and sickness, through plenty and want, through joy and sorrow, now and forever.

Wedding Vow 4

I take you........................., to be my (husband/wife), loving you now and as you grow and develop into all that God intends. I will love you when we are together and when -we are apart; when our lives are at peace and when they are in turmoil; when I am proud of you and when I am disappointed in you; in times of rest and in times of work. I will honor your goals and dreams and help you to fulfill them. From the depth of my being, I will seek to be open and honest with you. I say these things believing that God is in the midst of them all.

NOTE: Anyone of these vows shall be used for you during your wedding ceremony. Remember that these vows are powerful and holy as you exchange them in the presence of Almighty God; therefore, they must not be violated.

Wedding Speeches Sample

Groom's Speeches Sample

On wedding day, the Groom can be asked to make a short speech about his wife; how he met her, what made him to love her or what made him to decide to marry her. You should prepare for this before your wedding day.

Groom's Speech Sample 1

Today, I am happy that I married the woman of my dream. She is my best friend and lover, and thankfully, she is my wife. When we first met, I thought that she was just an ordinary woman but she was different. I quickly came to learn that she is also caring, compassionate and loyal. I feel extremely blessed to have **Mary** as my wife. I look forward to our life together, with all its twists and turns, joys and sorrows.
I love **Mary** forever with all my heart, mind and soul.

Groom's Speech Sample 2

Before I met **Anita**, I was moving with some other ladies but **Anita** is totally different from other ladies I moved with. She was a patient, hardworking and understanding lady. After a month I met her and have studied her, it dawned on me that I have found my exact life partner. I quickly took a decision to marry her and here we are today to make my decision and dream a reality. I love you my Angel.

Bride's Speeches Sample

The bride can also be asked to make a short speech on wedding day about what made her to accept the marriage proposal of her husband. You should also prepare for this before your wedding day.

Bride's speech sample 1

When **Mike** first approached me, I thought that he was not serious to go into a relationship with me. After six months, I saw the seriousness in him even at the point of proposing marriage to me. I could not still believe it until he fixed our wedding date and at the same time our traditional wedding date. I had no choice than to succumb to his desire since he is serious and at the same time, I love him.

Bride's Speech Sample 2

Among all the men that were admiring me, I saw **Tony** as a different man because he was caring, generous and loving. These became the qualities that made me to humbly and respectfully acknowledged his marriage proposal and I am very happy today that Tony has become my love, life partner and husband.

The Order of wedding Photography

You can decide to select what you want your photographer to achieve for you.

Wedding Photographs before the wedding day (at studio).

- Formal bridal portrait at studio-waist up and full length

Wedding Photographs before the wedding ceremony (at the bride's house.)

- Bride getting dressed

- Bride and mother in mirror - putting on veil

- Bride and maid of honor - adjusting something

- Someone's "hand on dress" dress detail

- Bride - full length (dressed)

- Bride - waist up

- Bride -looking out of a window

- Bride and mother - full length

- Bride and maid of honor, waist up

- Bride with father - full length

- Bride with father - waist up

- Bride with mother and father- full length.

- Bride with mother and father- waist up

- Bride with individual family members - waist up or full length

- Bride with anyone / everyone else of importance - waist up or full length

- Bride with bride's maids -lined up

- Bride with bride's maids - informal

- Bride and family getting in car to leave for church·

Wedding Photographs before the wedding ceremony (at the church)

- Groom with best man

- Groom with best man "getting away"

- Groom with all Grooms' men lined up

- Groom with Groom's men- informal

- Groom with Dad

- Groom with Mum

Wedding Photographs (at the wedding ceremony)

- Mother of groom being escorted down the isle

- Mother of bride being escorted down the isle

- Any grandmothers being escorted down the isle

- Bride and Father at the back of the church getting ready to go down the isle

- Groom and best man waiting at the alter

- Bride - informal portrait as she waits to come down the isle

- Groom's men and bride's maids coming down the isle Father and Bride coming down the isle

- Father giving away Bride

- Exchanging vows

- Exchanging rings

- The kiss

- Alter from back of church - eye level POV (long shot) Alter from back of church - eye level POV (close up of bride and groom)

- Alter from back of church - floor POV (long shot)

- Alter from back of church- floor POV (close up of bride and groom)

- Alter from balcony - floor POV (long shot)

- Alter from balcony - floor POV (close up of bride and groom)

- Various editorial shots of ceremony

- Shot of Bride and Groom being introduce as husband and wife

- Bride and Groom coming down the isle

- Mother of bride being escorted from seat

- Mother of Groom being escorted from seat Bride looking out window

- Bride and groom kissing at the back the of church

- Various shots or receiving line

- Rice throw long shot to show crowd

- Bride and Groom getting into the car to leave for pictures / reception

Wedding Photographs after the ceremony but before the wedding reception (at a park or church premises)

- Bride full length (formal)

- Bride waist up (formal)

- Bride with maid of honor

- Bride with bride's maids formal and informal

- Bride and groom -full length

- Bride and groom -waist up

- Bride and Groom with his parents

- Bride and Groom with her parents

- Bride and groom with each set of grandparents

- Bride and groom with bride's maids and groom's men two or three versions

- Groom with groom's men formal and informal

- Bride and Groom Editorial portraits together and separate use unique environment

Wedding photographs (at the wedding reception)

- Bride and groom being introduced at reception

- Individual table shots

- Best man toasting

- Group shot of all guests

- Cake alone

- Bride and Groom cutting cake

- Bride and Groom smashing cake

- The first dance

- Bride and her father dancing

- Groom and his mother dancing

- Bride's parents dancing

- Groom's parents dancing

- Bride and or groom dancing with grand parents

- Bride throwing bouquet

- Groom removing garter

- Groom throwing garter

- Garter catcher putting garter on bouquet catcher

- Groom carrying bride away

- Bride and groom getting into the car

- Car driving away

- Group shot of wedding guests

This is the normal order of wedding photography. If you have other special people that you want to take photograph with, add them to this list and notify your photographer.

The order of events at your wedding reception

- Guests Arrive at the Reception Site

- Introducing the wedding party

- Introducing the bride and groom

- Giving the blessing / prayer

- Sharing the food & drinks

- Cutting the cake

- Toasting the happy couple

- Bride & groom's first dance

- Father & daughter's dance

- Mother & groom's dance

- Special dances

- Bouquet and garter toss

- Dancing and fun

Note: The order of events listed above is just mere suggestions. You can choose to rearrange or modify them to suit your guests or your desire.

The explanation and details of the order of events at your wedding reception

Guests Arrive at the Reception Site: Some guests arrive early at the reception. So be sure all reception to-dos are complete by the time your wedding's scheduled to start. Also, all wedding vendors /ushers should be suited up in proper attire for early and lingering guests. All tables should be set up, including the cake table, the entertainment's table, the sign-in table, food tables, and tables with chairs for all guests. If you have a seating arrangements, all seating list should be at the reception with everyone's name indicating where they sit.

Introducing the Wedding Party: This step isn't mandatory, but it's nice for everyone to know who the wedding party are. Many guests haven't met them before your wedding. Create a "Reception Planning Guide," and give this to your emcee before the wedding. Among other things, this guide should detail your party by the order they enter the reception site, and give their names and titles. The order of entrance is: parents of the groom, ushers with bridesmaids, flower girl and ring bearer, special guests, best man, maid/ matron of honor, bride and groom. In addition, go over how to pronounce the wedding party's names with the emcee.

Introducing the Bride and Groom: This is always the last of the introductions. Everyone should stand before the bride and groom enter. In addition, you can arrange a special song with the musical entertainment and a special announcement with the emcee to punctuate a truly grand entrance. Also, inform the emcee how you'd like to be introduced: Mr. and Mrs. Smith? John and Jane Doe?

Giving the Blessing/ prayer: This is another step that's not mandatory- but for the religious couple, it makes a nice setting. If you invite the ministers to the reception, ask them to conduct the blessing. But if they're not able to attend, a parent or family friend is a good idea. Alternatively, the emcee could bless the meal. Be sure to communicate with whoever' `giving the blessing well in advance, so they're prepared to give it a personal touch.

Sharing the food & drinks: It's time to eat! And no matter how many people who are clamoring to wish you well, the bride and groom should stop, rest and partake. This may be your only chance in the day that can all-too-easily become one big blur. Plus, it's customary for the bride and groom to start the food line, which most guests are aware of-so don't be late!

Cutting the cake: Of course, the bride and groom traditionally cut the first slice on their wedding cake. Then, the bride feeds half of the piece of cake to the groom, and the groom feeds the remainder to the bride. The ceremonial cutting is meant to symbolize the couple's caring and sharing for one another. Don't be afraid to use forks for this step, since they look great in pictures. They almost minimize the possibility of smearing cake all over the wedding regalia. Some people may choose to cut the cake and share it before sharing the food. You can do this if you want it that way.

Toasting the Happy Couple: In the first stage of toasting, the bride and groom toast each other, then interlock arms and drink. Immediately following, the best man and maid/ matron of honor make toasts to the bridal couple. Be prepared for other family and friends to follow too.

Bride & Groom's First Dance: The Bride & Groom's Dance is the first dance between a bride and groom as a married couple. Where you choose to place this in the schedule depends on your preferences. One common option: immediately following the grand entrance, with the wedding party circling the dance.

Father & Daughter's Dance: The Father & Daughter's Dance or the father Bride Dance is the dance between the father(s) of the bride and the bride. Brides, if you have more than one father in your life, one can tap the other on the shoulder in the middle of the dance so you can dance with both of them. If you don't have a father, a common substitute is a father figure. Even your brother would make a very nice gesture.

Mother & Groom's Dance: The Mother & Groom's dance is the dance between the mother(s) of the groom and Groom If you have more than one mother in your life, one can tap the other on the shoulder in the middle of the dance so you can dance with both. If you don't have a mother, a common substitute is a mother figure, or your sister.

Special Dances: Like many people, you might have some songs that are near and dear to your heart. You can ask the entertainer to play them immediately after the formal dances, example: if someone close to you passed recently, you could ask the entertainment to play" Angels Among Us" by Alabama.

Bouquet and Garter Toss: In the traditional tossing of the bouquet, the bride tosses her bouquet (or a substitute) to all the single women in attendance. Immediately after the tossing, a chair is set in the middle of the dance floor, for the bride to sit on while the groom removes the garter from her leg, and tosses it to all the single men in attendance. The man and woman who catch the garter and bouquet are said to be the next to marry.

Dancing and Fun: This is what you pay the music entertainment to get people out of their chairs and on to the dance floor.

Wedding Invitation Wording Sample

Both Parents inviting Sample 1

Mr and Mrs Coker
and
Mr and Mrs Williams
Invite you to celebrate
The marriage of their children
Tina Coker and **Tony Williams**
On Saturday, 21st May 2008
@ St. Peter's Church 5, Brilla Road
London. At 10.00am.
Reception follows immediately
@ Sky Pavilion,
Brilla Road London.
by 12.00 noon.

Both Parents inviting Sample 2

The families of **Coker**
and
The families of **Williams**

Cordially Invite........................... to

celebrate

The marriage of their children

Tina Coker and **Tony Williams**
On Saturday, 21st May 2008

@ S1, Peter's Church 5, Brilla Road
London. At 10.00am.
Reception follows immediately
@ Sky Pavilion,
Brilla Road London.
by 12.00 noon.

<u>Both Parents Inviting Sample 3</u>

With the blessings of our Heavenly father
The families of **Alli** and
The families of **Ibe**
Invite you to celebrate
The marriage of their children
Lade Alli and **Ike Ibe**
On Saturday, 21st May 2008
@ St. Peter's Church 5, Brilla Road
London. At 10.00am.
Reception follows immediately
@ Sky Pavilion, Brilla Road

Both Parents Inviting Sample 4

With the blessings of our Heavenly father
Mr and Mrs **Jones**
and
Mr and Mrs **Mensah**

request your presence at the
Wedding celebration of their children
Cynthia Jones and **Edwin Mensah**
On Saturday, 21st May 2008
@ St. Peter's Church 5, Brilla Road
London. At 10.00am.

Reception follows immediately
@ Sky Pavilion, Brilla Road London.
by 12.00 noon.

<u>Both Parents inviting Sample 5</u>

The families of
Chief & Chief (Mrs) Alli
and
Mr & Mrs Ibe

Cordially invite you to celebrate
The marriage of their children
Lade Alli and **Ike Ibe**

On Saturday, 21st May 2008
@ St. Peter's Church 5, Brilla Road
London. At 10.00am.

Reception follows immediately @ Sky
Pavilion, Brilla Road London
by 12.00 noon.

Note: You can put the names of your R.S.V.P,
Father of the day, Mother of the day, Sponsor
etc. You can also include the names of other
important personalities.

Thanking the guests who attended your wedding

After your wedding, it is your duty to show appreciation to those people who attended your wedding and equally gave you gifts. In the natural way, you can visit them in their homes and thank them but since many of them don't live near, you may need to prepare thank you notes and send to them.

Hopefully you have a neat list of gifts and the names of the people who gave them to you.

Thank you notes wording sample

Sample 1

Dear Aunt May and Uncle John,

We are so excited to receive your gift the other day. The crystal vase is gorgeous, and just the right size for our dining room table. I've already filled it with lilies. Thank you so much for your thoughtful and generous gift.

We look forward to seeing you on our big day!

Sincerely,
....

Sample 2

Dear Suzy,

You know how much I like a good martini, and now I can have 8! Thank you for the beautiful set of cocktail glasses. They are stylish and fun and we can't wait to throw a little party in their honor. As soon as we're back from our honeymoon, you'll have to help test out all the new bar recipes from the book you sent as well.

Can't wait! Thanks again
Love,

....

Sample 3

Dear Rachel and Tom,

Thank you so much for the Tiffany glasses. Those glasses were one of the first things Anthony and I registered for because we both loved them immediately. Now whenever we use them we will think of you! Thanks also for helping make our big day so special. It was wonderful to see you there.

Best wishes,

....

Sample 4

Dear Lisa and Ted,

We've already used your stackable mixing bowls several times! They're incredibly useful. I honestly don't know what I've been doing without them. Thank you for the thoughtful and helpful gift.

Thanks also for sharing our wedding day. Having you there made it extra-special! .

Much love,

....

Note: When you are writing thank you letter, it will be nice if you indicate how importance or useful that gift was or is to you. It will make the giver to be happy that the gift he or she gave to you is useful to you.

Important facts about wedding

- The meaning of wedding is joining or uniting. Therefore, after wedding, you have been joined or united together.

- The most important aspect of wedding is the exchange of vow and ring which brings about the unity, commitment and love.

- You should think of the happiness and love that should last after your wedding and not the extravagant spending for it.

- The happiness you were during your wedding should remain after your wedding.

- Your wedding should be planned according to your financial capacity.

- There is nothing wrong if you wed with somebody who is not from your tribe, state or country. What is important is the love and understanding that both of you have for each other.

- Some people spend the whole money they have to plan a big wedding and start starving· after the wedding. This is not the best.

- Some People go about borrowing money to plan a big wedding and become debtors after the wedding. This is not the best.

- You Ladies! When you attend someone's wedding and notice how extravagantly money was spent, you would wish your own wedding to be like that. Note that all fingers can never be equal.

How you can remain happy after your wedding

- The vows that both of you exchanged in the church are made in the presence of God and they must not be violated. Every time in your lives keep on remembering those vows and as you do this, both of you will keep on living peacefully and happily.

- The rings that both of you exchanged are used to join both of you together so that you will become one in the presence of God. $(1 + 1 = 1)$ As both of you have become one now, anything that affects one person affects the other. If one person is happy, the other is equally happy. Always bear it in mind that both of you are now one.

- The people who were at the church to witness two of you being joined with the ring have discovered that both of you have been joined in the presence of God and therefore, nobody should put asunder.

- The first piece of cake that both of you ate at the reception symbolizes your first meal together. Both of you should continue eating together until death separates you.

- The grain which the cake is made of stands for fertility and fruitfulness in your marriage.

- The joy of marriage is children, if your wife is delaying or failing to bear children, do not humiliate her yet until you discover the cause of the problem. Some times, men can be the cause of failing to bear children in marriages.

- If your wife is giving birth to only female children, please do not humiliate her, do not allow your family members also to humiliate her, she is surely not the cause.

- Quarrel must come between two of you but try to settle it amicably without inviting a third party.

- Both of you should not be angry at the same time.

- The wife should be submissive to her husband who is the head of the family.

- At least once every day try to say complimentary or romantic thing to your life partner.

- If you have done something wrong, always admit it and ask for forgiveness and when you forgive your partner, never bring up that mistake or wrong doing any longer.

- If you have to criticize the other partner, do it lovingly.

I wish you happy married Life!

About the Author

Desmond Ihenze is a wedding specialist and event manager. He has helped many couples to plan their weddings.

Planning a wedding is interesting but at the same time, it has never been easy for many couples. On many occasions, most couples forget certain things, items or procedures that suppose to feature in their weddings due to the stress, tension and confusion that go with wedding planning.

This book is written to help couples plan their weddings successfully.

www.ingramcontent.com/pod-product-compliance
Lightning Source LLC
Chambersburg PA
CBHW071239280526
45787CB00002B/997